Gunshot, Peacock, Dog

Poems

Also by Rick Campbell:

A Day's Work

Setting the World in Order

The Traveler's Companion

Dixmont

The History of Steel

Gunshot, Peacock, Dog

Poems

Rick Campbell

MADVILLE PUBLISHING
LAKE DALLAS, TEXAS

FIRST EDITION

Requests for permission to reprint or reuse material from this work should be sent to:

Permissions
Madville Publishing
PO Box 358
Lake Dallas, TX 75065

Acknowledgements:
10x3 Plus: "Finding Everett Ruess"
ABZ: "A Small Poem for James Wright"
Alabama Literary Review: "Heart of Dependent Arising"
Apalachee Quarterly: "Working the Mountain, Encampment, Wyoming"
Cave Wall: "Love Would Burn On Through the Night"
Cork Literary Review: "Gunshot, Peacock, Dog"
Evening Street Review: "West Virginia" (as "Marker, West Virginia")
Fourth River: "A Theory of Humours," "Verbs for Armadillos," "Sitting In the Emergency Exit Row,"
        "Philosophy Made Simple"
Gargoyle: "Elegy in a Small Town Churchyard," "Night Boating On the Lake,"
        "Texas Highway Good Night," "Waiting for the Piggly Wiggly"
Iodine: "Ransom" and "Desire"
Kestrel: "Bird Eggs in the Propane Tank" and "One Day's Work in the Donut Shop"
Normal: "Gunshot, Peacock, Dog"
San Pedro River Review: "Pittsfield Train" and "Letter to Hugo from Hog Park Reservoir"
Snake Nation Review: "Wild Nights, Wild Nights" (as "Ohio Night") and "Cattle Egrets" (as "A
        Hundred Egrets")
Story South: "How to Save a Life," "A Map of My Body," "Lillian Spring Road," "The Crying Baby
        Flight," "Time of Death"
The Chattahoochee Review: "My First Transvestite"
The Florida Review: "Rainbow on Winding Creek" and "The Hour When Solomon Comes"
The Parthenon Review: "You Can't Go Home Again" (as "Palm Beach County, 1972")
The Autumn House Anthology of Contemporary Poetry: "Heart of Dependent Arising"

Thanks to Donna J. Long for her exceptional proofreading and wise editorial suggestions.

Cover Design: Jacqueline Davis

ISBN: 978-1-948692-04-5 Paper, 978-1-948692-05-2 ebook
Library of Congress Control Number: 2018948231

For Robert Dana (1929-2011)
My brother, Mick (1956-2010)
and
Della Rose Campbell, always, with all my love . . .

Contents

IV

V

They say every man needs protection
They say every man must fall

—Bob Dylan

Gunshot, Peacock, Dog

Poems

I

Sitting In the Emergency Exit Row

I answer that I am willing and able
to operate the emergency exit

but I have not listened for years
to any instructions.

I look at the exit hatch's
simple pictography

and remember my chronic
inability to assemble

cheap furniture, the dremel
tool, and my stupidity

when faced with the digital
camera's many settings.

I have agreed to save my life
and theirs—to keep from harm

the three toddlers sitting behind me.
I think of today's flight path

Louisville to Orlando, and I'm
grateful we will not fly

over gulf or ocean. It's hard
enough to promise expertise

opening this hatch
without admitting my slim chance

of swimming to any shore. We
cross the Ohio and I sigh

for one obstacle gone. I measure
my obligations topographically.

I'm one river closer to the tarmac,
one suburb closer to keeping this promise

to an airplane full of strangers.
There's snow on the hills and pastures.

Below, somewhere, coal mines,
and miners' wives in church.

Now I've done it again. Taken
the care of souls in my hands.

I could be a better steward. I slide
toward uselessness. Promises implied,

promises maybe never made,
gone now. The long list

of reasons I could change my seat
includes my *inability to orally*

impart information to other passengers.
The child behind me touches my elbow.

All I can hope for them now is luck.
I close my eyes and lean my head

on the bulwark, on the sign
marked Exit.

How to Save a Life

I don't remember much of it.
My father must have been at work.
Early afternoon, by the light, and across the street, Ivan,
our neighbor, home. He worked
three to eleven. I say my little brother went
to get him and I stayed with her. Ivan
or Celie or someone said *keep her walking. Don't
let her sleep.* How did they know?
Who tried to overdose on pills in their world?
Maybe they saw it on TV. I
walk her round and round the living room
until my father and the police come.
I remember feeling that everyone was watching, that
my father was not surprised, but Sammy, sad.
Keep her walking, that's all I really know.
When they take her away, don't forget her. Love
her anyway. Don't think about why.

A Map of My Body

The upper regions mapped, X,
Sharpie on masking tape in the center
of my throat. The machine traverses
a line, coordinates tied to this mark,
to other known points—clavicle,
jaw bone, maybe an ear lobe.
How far is this X from the scar
on my neck where my cancer
began? How far,

just for nostalgia, from the nose,
thirty years ago smashed by
the more tangible violence of a brick.
I've measured too often, the girth
of my waist, my weight, this last May
my wife's heartbeat, her breathing, as she lay
hooked to tubes and meters, whirling
and beeping. I measured her breath
by breath, diastole, systole, diastole,
systole. And even that highest of science
or art, that tick by tick connection
to the numbers of her blood, the difficulty
of breath, told me what matters
is immeasurable. Today

my mask fit tighter on my forehead,
and nose, and I feared something
had shifted. But my body—mapped now
like the plat that defines our home,
a point in concrete north of the driveway,

an iron pipe in the confluence of two creeks,
the angle between them—flat on this table
could be a job I worked years ago, painting
survey targets on the suburban streets
of Boca Raton. The laser burns my body,
maps what it is I am now: the chance
of my being someone else by summer,
the science of resurrection.

Elegy in a Small Town Churchyard

There are many born again or dreaming
of it, another lot wishing
their frailty would end. What

if I were smitten today
under this dogwood tree, moss
dangling in my car window.

You think I mean death? What of love,
of revelation? The church is quiet.
A lawn mower breaks the Sabbath

but all the birds are singing holy. We could
make too much of this or, more likely, find
it just the end of another day. *Lord*,
you might say, then again, maybe not.

Working the Mountain, Encampment, Wyoming

for my father (in a way)

I didn't tell him that this work
that I took from sheer need
had become a kind of love. That
the last day, moving seven tons of dirt,
singing like a fool, I did for me
and him. He always wanted a worker
who came home with a sore back,
and fell asleep on the floor.

I didn't tell him either
that this summer of shovels
had become the life we never had.
Even when the phone rang
a month later and said that his heart
                        was splayed open.

So I'd shoveled tons of dirt,
hauled more tons of rock, woke
in the dark Wyoming morning,
July ice on the truck windows
and walked out to work another day.
It wasn't the first time I sweated
a dirty job, first time I worked some place
with a name he'd never heard of, quit
before he found it on a map. I didn't explain
this one, but it's still there: gabion baskets
shoring a mountain, marking our lives
                        in silence and wind.

My Uncle's Hunting Trailer

1950's Airstream, well-made, not like the junk
my mother lives in. You take a pistol, gleaming

like a moccasin, from a blonde cabinet and we walk
through the cornfield to a line of locust trees

where you set a can on a stump. I don't remember
pulling the trigger, but the pistol kicked hard,

the air exploded; I missed the can. Maybe crows
whirled away, maybe wind rustled stalks. One shot

was enough, made me remember standing
at attention with the Junior Legion Drill team

as fathers fired their twenty-one gun salutes
on patriotic holidays. Despite my attempt to stay

stiff, my heart always flinched. I didn't tell you
any of this. You were a good man. We went

back to the trailer and soon your Jeep was heading
back to the town we once called home.

Driving Tevebaugh Hollow

On one side a small creek.
On both sides locust hills rise.
Sunlight trickles down broken shafts.

Where the hollow widens, derricks
rust in briers and vines.
They pumped thick crude

before Texas gushers and Gulf oil spills.
Nothing moves today but my rental car
rising from the river to Ridge Road

where I meld into October
trees blazing red and gold,
and join the highway to Mars.

Night Boating On the Lake

I imagine my stepbrother's body
tangled in willow or whatever scrub
comes down to the lake's shore.

Early spring, water winter cold.
Most trees still without leaves.
Does a body float after three days

or does the cold keep
it down? Do I remember
any of this true? There's this:

he died. He was young.
He was drunk. His promise
already gone.

Reclamation, to climb up from where
he'd fallen, was all he had.
It's too hard for most.

He fell one last time. The shore's
scattered yellow lights might have
called him; his friends, if sober,

might have found him. He could
have used just a little more luck.
It's a long way for a lost man to swim.

Ransom

What do you have of value? the kidnapper
whispers. I have land and trees, I say.
Not enough.
I have plums, cucumbers,
and tomatoes. *Not enough,* they say.

I have two cars. *Not enough,*
we have a fleet. I have five dogs.
No, the barking will give
us away.

I have a little money.
No. We have more than we need.

I have books, many books, and I have
ideas and words and notes. *No.*
No one wants those anymore.

I have little else but love
and now sorrow & loss.
Sorrow & loss, they say. *That's what*
we want. Send it on the wings
of buzzards & in the bellies of moccasins.

Send it all to us. Your family
is in the next room, sleeping.

Streetwise, Daytona Beach

We're walking the Boardwalk.
My young girlfriend's naïve
about the ways of cons and carnies,
and the pea beneath its tempting cup.
I'm showing off—been to Vegas, San Fran,
LA, hitched ocean to ocean. I've forged checks,
shoplifted, sold some weed; I'm in college
now, read Frye on heroes
and irony, so I toss my twenty
on the table, watch the whirling cups
with an attention my daily life rarely sees.

When I'm wrong I'm stupid again.
I'm sure no woman will love me. But
my young girlfriend doesn't leave me
and that night we make love
for a long sweet time. Maybe
she knows more than I believe in.
Maybe she loved me the only way
we could then: for the moment
until those moments end.

Peacocks in July

Max and his friends
sit on his porch
and his truths
float through the woods

Man you don't know shit
about melons. Last winter
was so cold the oranges
never set. Garlic's
almost cured. You see
Calvin's new goats?
The peacocks melt away.
Humidity's green and thick.
Everything rises and shimmers

Heart of Dependent Arising

for M

She's rolled into surgery
and as the drugs wash over her
she tries to remember her
Medicine Buddha meditation.
Her heart is still at the center
of her chest, the lotus flower
still eight-petalled and white.

The Healing Buddha, though
his light's still blue, has begun
to float off his moon disc. The
icons that surround him: *Actualized
Wisdom, Simultaneous Wealth*
are only colors now. But *Peacock's
Throat,* she remembers. Remembers
too—blissful, radiant light.

I figure this is enough
to let her go with the nurses
to the hands and scalpel
of her Georgia gynecologist
who yesterday told us
that the ovary is the size of a pecan.
I am left to sit in the cafeteria
with pager 209—that will flash
and beep when her doctor wants me.

We go for refuge to the Buddha.
We go for refuge to the empty clarity
of our minds. She prays too,
to the Virgin, but skips
in the hour of our death.

I have echoed our doctor's mantra
that this surgery is routine, a quick
in and out. But nothing
to the terminally anxious
is routine; anesthesia's two percent
death rate looms in her thoughts.

She dislikes hospital staff's blanket
reassurances and rolls
to surgery with yak bone *mala*
twisted in her right hand,

her Immaculate Heart of Mary scapula
wrapped around her wrist.
My pager blinks every three seconds
like a slowed heart beat,

and I wait in the secular world
I've made for myself through subtraction,
through sloughing off catechism, prayer,
Jesus, God, the saints and archangels.

I've nothing left but sin and hope.
A resolute faith in whom and what I love.
Many paths in a wood.
Many shafts of light.

II

My First Transvestite

(After Robert Hayden)

Boston diner, late winter night.
"Where you from," she asked. "Pittsburgh."
"Well, get on a bus and go." Before I could ask
Steve kicked me under the table. He
wasn't pretty, my first transvestite.
What did I know of such lovely
and lonely offices, of desire
so complete? My first transvestite left us
or maybe we left her. The night was always
young then. We climbed Bunker Hill
a few hours before dawn. Steve explained
transvestites. Why Pittsburgh, I asked.
Why the bus? My first transvestite
was not my last. None sang to me ever again,
but one night I heard Wainwright's
Have You Ever Been to Pittsburgh,
my first transvestite's song. I thought of him,
of her; it was winter then too and the night
came down cold and long.

Verbs for Armadillos

Skulk. Maraud. Plunder.

Morning, we enter the garden
and survey their effects—mulch
and straw pushed aside, holes
dug for grubs. It's not the rooting
of hogs, or the long scar of a backhoe,
but we fenced and fortified
against their hunger and hunger
always wins.

Fence. Fortify. Encase. Enclose.

I walk the fence
looking for signs of tunneling
and think of Steve McQueen.
Find likely spots, where fence
does not meet the ground, where magnolia
leaves are crushed, and pine straw driven
into the soil. I carry scraps of fencing,
a roll of baling wire, my fence pliers
and set to work mending, digging
this patch of fence below the earth.

Damage. Ravage. Destroy. Dismember.

The armadillos' monthly damage
isn't worth all the worry, the cutting
and twisting, nicks on my knuckles,
this beating of our breasts. Late
in summer there's little for them
to damage, but the idea of their breaching
our fences, their inevitable coming
defeating all our superior effort
makes us cry *damn them*

and talk of trapping, of mothballs,
of panther pee. Then I piss
along the fence.

I think of leaving the dogs out all night
and living out there with them: flashlight,
machete, baseball bat, waiting.
We will be a legion of armadillo hunters.
We'll need some moon—half to full
so that everything beyond sight
is not black, not past the edge of the earth.
We will sit and listen, then attack—
dogs and I coming down on the dillos
like Braveheart, faces painted blue.
The dogs run the dillos down,
rip their soft bellies open.
I get the slow ones, club them
like melons.

Decamp. Draggle. Deface. Debauch.

What good will this carnage do?
Our small force of four may win one night
but they are an army, reinforcements
across the creek, beyond the hills.
Count the dead on the roadside
and imagine battalions still to come.
How many nights can we foreswear sleep
for killing, before we are not fit to live
in our own house?

We might sit and dream of slaughter,
but fencing and mending, lamentation
and curses, that's more our way.
So we sleep all night with windows closed,
and the AC on; the dillos *dance,*
dawdle, gore and grub.

A Small Poem for James Wright

One afternoon in thick fog and summer
rain, I climbed out of a preacher's car
near Parkersburg, draped

my orange poncho over me and drifted
north like a bobbing traffic cone.
I hitched your river road toward

Martin's Ferry where the beautiful
autumn bodies threw themselves
at each other in the suicidal lights.

I never made it that time. Night
fell in Sistersville and an old woman
who harbored runaways, kids whose

fathers beat them and suffered other
sundry problems, called me off the street,
gave me a meal and a place to sleep.

The next morning, I said enough
to homage and hitched into the valley
and the refrigerator that waited for me there.

I knew where to find you.
Time was still on my side.

Archeology

I have come a thousand miles
for this. J&L's ruins, a gravel plain
on the Ohio's west bank. There's little
left but an archeology of memory—smokestacks,
ovens, foundry, smelter, slag. Someone
might ask what happened here? What brought
this culture to ruin? Drought? Pox?
Broken dreams? Who lived in ash
and cinder at the base of the great fires?
What twisted iron to scrap and left it to rust?
My inventory: butts, pull tabs, bolts, washers,
pencil stubs, bottle caps, screws, nails,
bones, rubbers, keys, our lives. I drop
a tarnished watch fob and broken penknife
in my pack and walk away.

Lillian Spring Road

This morning it was alive
when it came out of shadow—
brown mutt, brown trees, brown
grass in the swale—walked
in front of the car like a shopper
decides beans would be good for dinner
and turns casually toward the shelf.

I don't swerve as much as hope
for the center line. I don't want to spatter
my daughter on the grill of the Chevy
in the narrow lane beside me.
I hold a short breath until the dog
thumps my bumper and still I hope
that we—or the dog—are blessed, lucky,
and that death today might be like baseball,
a game of inches.

In the ditch it lay still—big ugly head,
maybe pit bull and chow, scarred legs, mange,
no collar. I let my breath out.
This dog, dead, no one will mourn.
No one call its name.

I left it there, winter falling on us,
and drove past the alfalfa field,
twenty rolls of hay, tractor
rusting near a derelict barn.

Bird Eggs in the Propane Tank

This is how you come into the world.
A nest of pine straw in the crown
of a gas tank. Below your snug
shelter a gauge reads volume,
copper hoses couple. A white
metal hut keeps you out of the rain,
safe enough. When I checked
our gas supply, there you slept
the sleep of the dead, the sleep
of the near living. Which
would it finally be?

I don't touch you, afraid of what
I think is true and probably isn't,
that your mother will abandon you
if I do. I promise to come back
and see what remains. What evidence
there is of your life, your death.
What story begins or ends here

Vulture

Vulture's not owl nor omen.
Don't ask what it means.
Vulture's no blessing,

though his work
must be done.
Inspect the road's

smeared guts, there's beetles,
ants, maggots; all, like vulture,
working an economy

that begs little from us
but fast cars driving
the killing floor.

A Theory of Humours

For M

She brings me fennel scones.
It's been years now since we worried
about the worm of sadness.

My wife without her spleen,
without the black bile
that quickened medieval

gloom. Friends barely knew
of her travail, yet the rare reader
who may have seen my chronicles

will wonder at this woman now.
Let me tell you all that some sort
of resurrection of the spirit, some

drop of healing light
from the far edge of death's dark
tunnel

or, if you believe, and given all
that you do believe why should you
doubt

that without her spleen to pump
her ruin, she's risen above her own
dungeon, shaken her demons loose.

Why should you discount Galen:

"the humour, like a darkness, invades the seat
of the soul wherever reason is situated. For
this reason the melancholiacs are afraid of it
and wish for it at the same time."

Why believe that a mark on the door
turns away god's wrath, that seven
is luckier than eight?

My wife, whom you met sad
is well now. Come to us and see.

Meet her in the garden where gourds
swell on a ladder trellis, and tomatoes
ripen long past July's consuming heat.

Sorry

Eskimos have a hundred words for snow
and men more for *sorry.*

There's a path into the woods,
but none back out.

There's a hill steeper than it seems,
a creek that in some other age

cut a channel too deep to wade. There's
lightning closer than the thunder says,

a copperhead you thought an oak.
Less passing lane than you need.

You see where this is going
but you go anyway. *Sorry*

Peacocks in the Winter Woods

Peacocks have no desire for silence
or stealth. They walk upright

like men sure the world
will do them no harm.

They march and wail,
ten abreast, point and flank,

no one too far ahead or behind.
We watched them high step

down the dappled hill where Sam,
hundred pound killer of deer,

feared by our pit bull neighbor
paced, barked, then just sat and stared.

The peacocks ignored him, trusted
the safe pass the fence promised.

III

Waiting for the Piggly Wiggly

Not, as in sleeping in line for a Harry Potter movie,
but drive-by waiting, discussing the future.
When will the new Piggly Wiggly open?
The Piggly Wiggly looks nothing like a pig,
but a warehouse, or new Baptist or Congregational
churches bent on proving God don't give a shit
about looks when talking to his chosen ones.
Nothing spent on design, no caving in to the esoteric
and no doubt more costly notion of beauty. Piggly
will house cheap groceries and we will come because
the Winn Dixie's old and dirty. Each day we drive
by Wiggly. First bulldozed dirt, then beige metal skeleton,
a nice black asphalt parking lot. It's big and optimistic
and there's no costly trees or plants. We say
it will be nice to have a new grocery store, even
if we have to say Piggly Wiggly Piggly Wiggly
more than we thought possible. O Piggly,
your aisles will gleam the first few months.
What you lack in sophistication
you'll lack in other areas too: fresh
fruit, customer service, squid, Guinness,
parmigiano-reggiano. Piggly Wiggly,
we will come to you anyway. Forsake what little
we had, forget our grander dreams, until
your floor too turns dingy.

Cattle Egrets

1.

in a new mown field of hay.
I drive east; the flock feasts this Sunday
morning, white smocks glinting
in the graying grass. Li Po
could make a poem of this. Loved
ones far away, down river after river,
in a land remembered by the last snow
and a moon white in the violet sky.

2.

Sometimes an egret is just an egret,
the pasture, someone else's land. What
could bring us here if not this highway?
What could keep us from this field,
its beetles, crickets, and worms, but duty,
our loved ones in the car, and our more sophisticated
palette? Egrets shimmer in the rear view mirror,
the rising heat—mirage, maybe dream.

The Crying Baby Flight

We are landing in the night
and the lights make our town a city,
the way one light in the dark
seems like home, seems safe.
The babies were brown and cried
loud in the native tongue of babies,
not the one their father used when he said
what no doubt meant *be quiet little one*
or *shut the fuck up* (and who among us
would know, though many of us were
thinking it). Then the baby said
I have to pee pee. I have to pee pee.
And we wanted to say *Jesus man,
let the kid pee*, but we were landing
and none of us could move and I
imagined a river of pee moving under
my seat, soaking my computer bag,
gliding toward the pilot's locked door.
Threat code yellow. Threat code warm.
I raised my feet; the baby was quiet,
his father too.

Texas Highway Good Night

*Abandoned by commercial hunters, the rescued baby buffaloes
later made up the Goodnight buffalo herd, which became
well known throughout the world.*
          —Lindsey Howald

The Goodnight moon rides herd
over brindled trailers. I'm almost asleep
in this rest area, but in my dreams or not
cattle are lowing and a stockyard stench
seeps through my van.

For their last
Sun Dance, Kiowa hunters had to buy
a buffalo somewhere across these sage hills
on the Goodnight ranch.

                    Morning shows
me cattle trucks parked where none
were last night. This is travel.

                I live here
where the centerline is the future
and I talk too much to the face
in the window, not the Hitchhiking
Jesus, but me. *You might be crazy*
the face says, *talking to your face
as it floats over the violet land.*
Maybe I'm driving home, I say.
Or just driving?

              Goodnight made a movie
in 1916 and invited the Kiowa
to one more buffalo hunt. Like
the old days, he said. *Nothing*
                    ends this way.

Race Relations in America

The *Eat Mo Chicken* cow
wanders the food court
dressed in black and white.
Everyone loves him.
Counter women at the Greek
fast food place hold babies
                up to be kissed.

We love this: people dressed
as cows, pigs, bunnies. Even
sausage and kielbasa figures
cajoling the box seats
we would invite home
to dinner, ask them to marry
                our sisters.

We would be good people,
fine citizens; our better angels
would shine through us if we waddled,
eyes large as panda's, fixed ever-open,
if we were cloaked and masked, fuzzy and huge,
if we traded our opposable thumbs
and trigger fingers for clumsy paws.

With smiles stitched on our faces,
oh the little dances we would do.
Make me a bunny, a mouse, a dog
with goofy ears. I will love all
the huggable strangers, share
the dream of cows of many colors.

Letter to Hugo from Hog Park Reservoir

Dear Dick:

I stood at the head of the spillway
and vowed to fish honestly, to hook
each one fair, no snagging, no scooping
them out like a brown bear.

Sunset, trout slapped cement,
struggled against the grade of falling water,
until failing, they half-mooned back
into the creek. I watched my spinner

glimmer through dark water. All day
they'd driven for the world
that used to lodge behind earth
and rock, draining now to Cheyenne.

A brown leapt and landed
behind me. As it flopped
toward the pool I pounced on it.
Twenty inches, fat and heavy. Now

I confess. Dick, would you
who claimed degradation, the many
forms of desperation, have let it
slide back to the creek? I had a string

of trout heavier than I could carry.
What does this say for me now, when
what I want most is forgiveness?
Write me when you can.

You Can't Go Home Again

for Dale, Greg, Chris

We ran traverse surveys
in the western county, out where
flood canals drained

the Everglades. We walked
fields of gladiolus waving
on green stalks. Herons

waded; kites and osprey soared
above a sea of yellow, pink
and white. We were just measuring

what was there—how far
from canal to canal. How low
the low lying land. I marked

boundaries, placed targets
for aerial surveys, turned angles
under banana spiders that floated

the power wires. 441 ran to Miami.
It seemed innocent. Were we too young
to see that what we fed developers

would bulldoze flower farms, breed
subdivisions and malls. Our work
wastes west of the Turnpike now.

The river of grass
long ago dreamed
its coming.

Peacocks Christmas Eve

When the peacocks sing night's
not silent anymore. Off key
caterwauling—like drunks caroling

who can't sing sober. Maybe
it's the dark moon, not the Savior's
birth, that panics them this winter night.

Why am I listening? These wailing
fowl are my prophets. I can't
avoid this ineluctable personification

though I know it's me who's desperate tonight.
Maybe the peacocks are just hungry or lost.
There's a coyote out there somewhere

following a star; the peacocks move
in a troop, safety in numbers, and even
the drunken hunters are home tonight.

Silent Night. Holy Night.
Let nothing I dismay.

Jesus at the Auction

Do I hear a dollar for this Jesus?
Never been on a dashboard.

Surely there's one among you who
will give a dollar, a small sacrifice,

to start the bidding. We've more fine
collectibles to come—Barbie

still in her box, Transformers—but
first let's tend to Jesus. Friends

don't miss this chance.
Just a dollar for Jesus.

Desire

I would be Billy Virdon
in the outfield next to Roberto.

I would be the river
so I would know trout.

I would be the moonflower
that wants to know the morning glory.

I would be Longfellow
so I could secretly envy Whitman.

I would be white bread
wanting to be rye.

I would be the mockingbird
dreaming of the tanager.

I would be all songbirds
singing for hawks.

I would be the whitetail bounding
toward heaven as I cross the creek.

My words could make another world;
we'd go on making, seeing, breathing.

ineluctable, intangible, infinite.

One Day's Work in the Donut Shop

My friend needed someone to make donuts.
Just one day, or maybe more if I wanted
it—a career in sugar and flour. Jess was a donut
king. He owned a franchise, and if he and his
wife worked thirty hours a day for the rest
of their lives, they could have the good life
in the new suburbs. I thought I could use
the money a morning of kneading dough
would bring, and I had nothing else to do
at six a.m., or any other time of day.
My life was often like that. I was warned
not to eat the frosting and the crèmes.
It was disgusting—the empty donuts
waiting to be shot up with fillings, the sweet
cake dough, all of it clinging to my fingers.
By ten I was sick. My lumpy, sweet
stomach and I said no thanks to the offer
of another day, no thanks to the bag
of free donuts. No thanks, I guess,
to the good life too—its creamy center.

Pittsfield Train

As the sun sank they came. Men
in railroad caps, women and children.
They knew every switch from Boston
to Albany, knew which engineer
rode the throttle heavy to make up
lost time.
                    They eyed us
as dusk fell. We were passengers.
Tonight the train stopped for us. They
circled our bags, little ones tried to touch
my long hair. I chanted

                    I will ride
your train. I'll watch the land fall away
from my window. I know the river's
moonlight silver. In the dark morning
my boots will grind the cinders of the Erie Station.

                    The terminal's quiet
at dawn. One old man sleeps under a paper.
A gray janitor mops the floor. I'll echo
through the room as the train pulls out
to Cleveland. I will never come again.

IV

Philosophy Made Simple

for Guy, Laramie, 1982

We were younger. Our mantra:
no matter what, you have to do
something next.

And we borrowed:
*You do what you must do
and you do it well.*

We were naïve
and didn't know enough
of loss and sorrow.

We didn't know
about being broken,
about wind and shattered

windows, dead childen,
fallow fields. We had
no rusting tractors,

no crushed legs, no smashed cars
in the swale, no lymphoma.
Even our nothing looked

like something. Days could pass
without love. Songs fade
away on radios. We lived

as if blessed: steam baths, coffee, beer,
meat pies and ball games in the Student Union.
It was easy to be fulfilled. Something

always happened next and we did not look
far enough into the dark to fear its coming.

Graveyard Shift

Wrapped in glass, each night
I knew I could die. Sea air
drifted in, coated the windows
of the self-serve gas station
where I sat, alone, on display.

The Unfortunate Worker

I sold coke, cigarettes, gas, but
really, sale signs all said *kill me.*
Who will know? Who will care?
No lights around. No other
stores. Dark. West
Riviera Beach, I-95.

Kill me tonight. Any night.
I listened to music, danced,
paced, then fell asleep.
Kill me. Each car
that came in could.

West Virginia

for Rosemary Campbell, 1924-1992

I wait for you
like a fisherman casting
to an eddy below a rock, certain
a trout holds there, dorsal fin beating slowly,
just enough to keep it hanging in the water
above the soft, rounded stones of the stream
bottom. Nights, I look for you
in your chair, some green cloth
draped across your lap. I hear
a clock ticking, cars braking the curve
on the hill, the dog dreaming loud.
This old pine house settles
          around me.

Tonight, there's ice on your Dunbar
streets, but I want to bundle off
to where the world ends—
the hills above the Kanawha
where we laid your body down.

Wild Nights, Wild Nights

for Johnny

Outside of forgotten small town
Ohio, the last time I saw you I was upside down,
your VW bus rolled in a ditch. I didn't like you

even before we almost died. Muted
light in a small hospital emergency room,
a doctor checks my head, holds up

fingers as I do simple math—two, three,
but I couldn't talk: some shock from being
drunk on Mickey's large mouth swill

and battered between bus
cabinets and the door. We lived
together once in the accident

of the 70s; you were a cheap little
shit, never sharing anything.
On my knees in the dirt, I see you

in the night's greasy light jumping
around like a rooster, throwing a bag
of pot, a tin of hash, your best clay pipes

into the brush, scared your small town
cops, lights flashing toward us,
might bust you.

I left the next day, east or south,
it didn't matter then. I could talk again,
but there was still nothing to say.

Finding Everett Ruess

Life does not grip me very powerfully in the present,
but I hope it will again.
—Everett Reuss

Everett Ruess' body was found on Comb Ridge,
Michael writes, and I think of Hugo's recipe
that all truth must conform to music. I
want to tell him that I love these words
into a line, that I hope he did not love
Ruess, that he writes this to me—
brief, enigmatic, without gloss—so
I will steal it.

I walked Comb Ridge once,
that day we left Ken at the motel.
The ridge, he said, would be too much for his failing
legs. Ken was dying. We didn't know
that already cancer had found his pancreas.
We walked that bleached whale bone
to where the Old Ones' ruins remained
in a wash, where rock overhung stones
piled to make a table, where a pestle,
maybe 700 years old, still holds corn.

It's not history if you can roll
the long past in your hands
and it clicks and rattles. Say to all,
for what it's worth, there's just then
and now, a string of sun and moon,
seasons of snow, hawks, sky, stars.
We worked our way out, followed terrain
like common sense and found ourselves
a mile from the car. Ken's dead.
Reuss too.

Sorrow School

Our text book has two lines

Is this what you wanted?
This is what you want.

Our teacher shape shifts:
tornado, drought, flood

Imagining is forbidden. We've
had no holiday in seven years

In physics we act out
the Uncertainty Principle

In shop we build useless boxes
In philosophy we discuss the epistemology

of Schrodinger's cat; history is
stuck in The Hundred Years War

In music we hum dissonance
Lit class is mired in semiotics

There is no graduation day.

In Our Almost Lost Dream

Something is burning on the horizon.
Maybe a grass fire, a small town
we once knew. Then we enter
the courtyard of a narrow mansion
with many skylights; starlight
falls as we walk room to room. At
the end of each hallway we turn right.
A blue door opens into a party.
A rich woman comes to us with crystal goblets
and says it's too bad your grandfather
had to play the benefit on River Street tonight.
We know, somehow, to say yes.

Time of Death

for Dean

Looking through the glass
as the doctors turned and walked
away, you knew there was no reason
to go on. This is the way the world
ends. What good is love
if it could not keep you both alive?
The last moments fall away like flakes of ash.
Her hand drops. Her children leave. Now
she too is gone. What's left?
A sky of grief, the long green Gulf sailing
away to the edge of the world? You, watching
it every day, all night, waking again, here?

The Hour When Solomon Comes

I buried five dogs here, wrapped them
in sheets and old shirts. When I laid
their bodies down, holes turned to graves.

I gentled shovels of dirt across their stiffening bodies.
Morning glories, lavender, mint.
Orange trees, persimmons, figs.

Sun rising slowly over tall trees.
Land falling to the creeks. There
never was a paradise, skeptics say.

Yesterday, on the campus where I work
a young eagle on a power pole keened
and cried. Mockingbirds dove, whirled, darted

in again and again. I needed to believe
the eagle cried for someone to save it.
I watched the gray sky north and south.

Rainbow Over Winding Creek Road

When the rain fell, fat drops
spattered my head. At the driveway
gate a blue rainbow arched over the dirt road;
beginning and end, both touched red earth.

I walked over in the name of science to see
if a man could pass through a rainbow
and come out the man he was. When
a man walks through a rainbow

he never returns, but lives in a place we can't name,
a land like witness protection. Nothing
that he was remains and nothing
that he is rings true. His daughter,

on the porch, waits and waits. The rain
stops. The sun sets. Darkness falls and her
dad never comes home. She gets cards posted
from towns that sound like Tulsa, Enid, Dumas,

Dalhart. Just pictures of cattle, fences, long skies,
thick clouds, no words, but in the bottom corner
a crude *fleur de lis*. She knows it's him. She
wants to believe he'll come back, that

he didn't just walk away in the rain. She
loves him, but he's afraid he lost that too
when sunlight shifted a few degrees west
and the rainbow she never saw was gone.

Gunshot, Peacock, Dog

There's a trick of topography
here. We sit on a hill and the sun's
below us, illusion I know. Sun,
green, and shadow roll
to the beech across the creek
shining in its own shaft of light.

This is not science. I read
RP's *Fugitive* poems, thirty years after
their season, and wonder what
will become of me. A shot breaks
the morning. The little dogs bark
and peacocks answer

their crazy cry of *why, why, save
me, save me.* I can't. This life
here, while good and blessed
by green and wind, falls slowly
to ruin. Eaves pocked by a mad
woodpecker, deck slick with mildew,

roof compromised. Muir's cat-briers
twist rampant in the woods and hydrangea
choke their neighbor trees. I've a list
of things to do which begins
with pay attention. Forty miles
from here, my brother twists

in his hospital bed, one leg
cut off, stump under the sheet,
                              the other dying.
I want to say that I love him
like these trees, like even
the distant peacock, but for years

he maddened me as he fell further
from health and purpose. There's
nothing left but mourn what's to come.
Maybe the peacocks' cry will do.
There's a dozen songbirds
and leaf rustle high in the trees.
If I sit here long enough
the redtailed hawk will keen.

V

Love Would Burn On Through the Night

for R. P. Dana

1.

I used to dance with my daughter
in my arms and sing her to sleep.
No Della no cry, no Della no cry.

You're dying and you know it,
entertaining pilgrims knocking
                              on your door.

I'm thinking of us standing
at your grave, then drinking
in a bar as we share stories.

*Good friends we have, oh, good friends
                        we've lost.*

When Della was four
she said "Daddy
no singing, just dancing."

2.

*In this bright future you can't forget your past
                    So dry your tears I say*

Where's the sorrow in this damn elegy?
I keep waiting for a dirge to beat,
for bereft women to tear

their hair, for all of us to weep in some
iambic choir. "Every day I live
I live forever," you said. Can't

cry for that line, and those shekinahs
you found in the Iowa clouds, they're
here now, coming to dwell in me

as if I'm some sacred tabernacle, some
vessel you've laid hands on.
                              Can't weep

yet, RP, there's more slapdash,
the lost whereafter. Call this an elegy
the way RP would like it.

Single malt. A good steak and all of us,
if I have my way, singing
the rest of the song

Everything's gonna be alright,
Everything's gonna be alright now

About the Author

Rick Campbell has published five previous collections of poetry and numerous poems and essays. He teaches in the Sierra Nevada College Low Residency MFA Program and at Florida A&M University. He lives on Alligator Point in Florida's Panhandle.

www.ingramcontent.com/pod-product-compliance
Lightning Source LLC
Chambersburg PA
CBHW022039090426
42741CB00007B/1130